Landscape Over Zero

For dear sheila

北岛
Bei Dao
Sep. 26, 98

Also by Bei Dao

POETRY

The August Sleepwalker (1990)
translated by Bonnie S. McDougall

Old Snow (1991)
translated by Bonnie S. McDougall and Chen Maiping

Forms of Distance (1994)
translated by David Hinton

SHORT STORIES

Waves (1990)
translated by Bonnie S. McDougall and Susette Ternent Cooke

BEI DAO

Landscape Over Zero

Translated by David Hinton
with Yanbing Chen

A NEW DIRECTIONS BOOK

Acknowledgments

Some of the poems in this book have appeared in the following periodicals:
Conjunctions, *Grand Street*, and *The Troubadour*.

Translation of this book was supported in part by the Witter Bynner Foundation.

Manufactured in the United States of America
New Directions books are printed on acid-free paper.
First published as New Directions Paperbook 831 in 1996
Published simultaneously in Canada by Penguin Books Canada Limited

Library of Congress Cataloging-in-Publication Data

Pei-tao, 1949–
    Landscape over zero / Bei Dao : translated by David Hinton, with
Yanbing Chen.
    p.   cm.
    A translation of 50 poems from the Chinese with no original title.
    Chinese and English.
    ISBN 0–8112–1334–X (alk. paper)
    I. Hinton, David, 1954–   II.   Chen, Yanbing.   III. Title.
PL2892.E525H56   1996
895.1'152—dc20   96–20854
                                                              CIP

Celebrating 60 years of publishing for James Laughlin
by New Directions Publishing Corporation
80 Eighth Avenue, New York 10011

目录　CONTENTS

To Shao Fei and Tiantian

零度以上的风景

Landscape Over Zero

抵达

那时我们还年轻
疲倦得象一只瓶子
等待愤怒升起

哦岁月的愤怒

火光羞惭啊黑夜永存
在书中出生入死
圣者展现了冬天的意义

哦出发的意义

汇合着的啜泣抬头
大声叫喊
被主所遗忘

ARRIVAL

we were still young then
tired as some bottle
waiting for anger to rise

o anger of the years

firelight shamed o dark night alive forever
migrating in books through life and death
sages reveal the meaning of winter

o meaning of going forth

gathering sobs look up
scream out
in their god's amnesia

另一个

这棋艺平凡的天空
看海水变色
楼梯深入镜子
盲人学校里的手指
触摸鸟的消亡

这闲置冬天的桌子
看灯火明灭
记忆几度回首
自由射手们在他乡
听历史的风声

某些人早已经匿名
或被我们阻拦在
地平线以下
而另一个在我们之间
突然嚎啕大哭

ANOTHER

this sky unexceptional at chess
watches the sea change color
a ladder goes deep into the mirror
fingers in a school for the blind
touch the extinction of birds

look at those flickering lights
on winter's fallow table
memory looks back a few times
the archer of freedom in foreign lands
listen to history's wind

some abandoned their names long ago
or we stalled them
under the horizon
meanwhile another among us
bursts into tears

蓝 墙

道路追问天空

一只轮子
寻找另一只轮子作证:

这温暖的皮毛
闪电之诗
生殖和激情
此刻或缩小的全景
无梦

是汽油的欢乐

BLUE WALL

road chases sky asking

one wheel
seeks another to bear witness

this pelt of warmth
poetry of lightning
procreation and passion
this very moment or whole vistas reduced
dreamless

are gasoline's thrills

创 造

世世代代的创造令我不安
例如夜在法律上奔走
总有一种原因
一只狗向着雾狂吠
船在短波中航行
被我忘记了的灯塔
如同拔掉的牙不再疼痛
翻飞的书搅乱了风景
太阳因得救而升起
那些人孤独得跺着脚排队
一阵钟声为他们押韵

除此以外还剩下什么
霞光在玻璃上大笑
电梯下降，却没有地狱
一个被国家辞退的人
穿过昏热的午睡
来到海滩，潜入水底

CREATION

all those generations being created rob me of peace
night for instance scurries around above the law
never without reason
a dog barks wildly at fog
ships sail on shortwave
the lighthouse I've forgotten
painless as a pulled tooth
fluttering books spoil the scenery
the sun rises salvaged
people there so lonely they stand in line stamping their feet
a bell tolling for them providing the rhyme

what is it remains beyond this
twilight laughs out loud on glass
the elevator decends, but there's no hell
someone the country's discharged
passes through a stifling-hot midday nap
reaches a beach, dives down deep

完整

在完整的一天的尽头
一些搜寻爱情的小人物
在黄昏留下了伤痕

必有完整的睡眠
天使在其中关怀某些
开花的特权

当完整的罪行进行时
钟表才会准时
火车才会开动

琥珀里完整的火焰
战争的客人们
围着它取暖

冷场,完整的月亮升起
一个药剂师在配制
剧毒的时间

PERFECT

at the end of a perfect day
those simple people looking for love
left scars on twilight

there must be a perfect sleep
in which angels tend certain
blossoming privileges

when the perfect crime happens
clocks will be on time
trains will start moving

a perfect flame in amber
war's guests
gather around it keeping warm

stage hushed, perfect moon rising
the pharmacist is preparing
a total poison of time

背景

必须修改背景
你才能够重返故乡

时间撼动了某些字
起飞，又落下
没透露任何消息
一连串的失败是捷径
穿过大雪中寂静的看台
逼向老年的大钟

而一个家庭宴会的高潮
和酒精的含量有关
离你最近的女人
总是带着历史的愁容
注视着积雪、空行

田鼠们所坚信的黑暗

BACKGROUND

the background needs revising
you can return to your hometown

a few time-shaken words
lift into flight, fall back
divulging no news whatsoever
a string of failures is the shortcut
past silent grandstands in heavy snow
pressing toward the huge clock of old age

at the family gathering
high tide is a matter of alcohol content
the woman closest to you
always wears the worried look of history
gazes into snowdrifts, double space to

darkness in which voles believe absolutely

无 题

在父亲平坦的想象中
孩子们固执的叫喊
终于撞上了高山
不要惊慌
我沿着某些树的想法
从口吃转向歌唱

来自远方的悲伤
是一种权力
我用它锯桌子
有人为了爱情出发
而一座宫殿追随风暴
驶过很多王朝

带家具的生活
以外, 跳蚤擂动大鼓
道士们练习升天
青春深入小巷
为夜的逻辑而哭
我得到休息

UNTITLED

in the plains of a father's imagination
insistent cries of children
strike high peaks in the end
don't panic
tracing thoughts of certain trees
I stutter into song

sorrow from far away
is a kind of power
I use it to saw tables
someone sets out for the sake of love
and a palace following storms
sails through many dynasties

beyond life with home
furnishings, fleas beat a huge drum
Taoists practice their ascent into heaven
youth goes deep into back alleys
weeping over the logic of night
I attain rest

这一天

风熟知爱情
夏日闪烁着皇家的颜色
钓鱼人孤独地测量
大地的伤口
敲响的钟在膨胀
午后的漫步者
请加入这岁月的含义

有人俯向钢琴
有人扛着梯子走过
睡意被推迟了几分钟
仅仅几分钟
太阳在研究阴影
我从明镜饮水
看见心目中的敌人

男高音的歌声
象油轮激怒大海
我凌晨三时打开罐头
让那些鱼大放光明

THIS DAY

wind knows what love is
the summer day flashing royal colors
a lone fisherman surveys
the world's wound
a struck bell swells
people strolling in the afternoon
please join the year's implications

someone bends toward a piano
someone carries a ladder past
sleepiness has been postponed a few minutes
only a few minutes
the sun researches shadow
and drinking water from a bright mirror
I see the enemy within

an oil tanker
the tenor's song enrages the sea
at three in the morning I open a tin can
setting some fish on fire

二月

夜正趋于完美
我在语言中漂流
死亡的乐器
充满了冰

谁在日子的裂缝上
歌唱，水变苦
火焰失血
山猫般奔向星星
必有一种形式
才能做梦

在早晨的寒冷中
一只觉醒的鸟
更接近真理
而我和我的诗
一起下沉

书中的二月：
某些动作与阴影

FEBRUARY

night approaching perfection
I float amid languages
the brasses in death's music
full of ice

who's up over the crack in day
singing, water turns bitter
bled flames pale
leaping like leopards toward stars
to dream
you need a form

in the cold morning
an awakened bird
comes closer to truth
as I and my poems
sink together

february in the book:
certain movements and shadows

进 程

日复一日，苦难
正如伟大的事业般衰败
象一个小官僚
我坐在我的命运中
点亮孤独的国家

死者没有朋友
盲目的煤，嘹亮的灯光
我走在我的疼痛上
围栏以外的羊群
似田野开绽

形式的大雨使石头
变得残破不堪
我建造我的年代
孩子们凭借一道口令
穿过书的防线

PROGRESS

day after day, misery
fails like some great venture
I sit within my fate
like a small-time bureaucrat
lighting a lonely country

the dead have no friends
blind coal, resonant lamplight
I walk above my pain
herds of sheep outside the fence
as if fields were breaking open

the heavy rains of form change stone
into utter ruins
I construct these our times
children using a password
penetrate the book's defenses

我 们

失魂落魄
提着灯笼追赶春天

伤疤发亮，杯子转动
光线被创造
看那迷人的时刻：
盗贼潜入邮局
信发出叫喊

钉子啊钉子
这歌词不可更改
木柴紧紧搂在一起
寻找听众

寻找冬天的心
河流尽头
船夫等待着茫茫暮色

必有人重写爱情

we

lost souls and scattered spirits
holding lanterns chase spring

scars shimmer, cups revolve
light's being created
look at that enchanting moment
a thief steals into a post office
letters cry out

nails o nails
the lyrics never change
firewood huddles together
searching for an audience to listen

searching for the heart of winter
river's end
a boatman awaiting boundless twilight

there must be someone to rewrite love

出　场

语病盛开的童年
我们不多说
闲逛人生
看栅栏后的大海
我们搭乘过的季节
跃入其中

音乐冷酷无比
而婚姻错落有致
一个厌世者
走向确切的地址
如烟消散

无尽的悲哀之浪
催孩子们起床
阳光聚散
我们不多说

SHOWING UP

in childhoods of broken grammar blooming
we don't say much
roam life
watch oceans beyond fences
seasons by which we traveled
plunge in

music perfectly cold and cruel
marriage neatly strewn
someone sick of this world
walks toward a definite address
like smoke vanishing

endless waves of sorrow
hurry children out of bed
sunlight gathers & scatters
we don't say much

在歧路

从前的日子痛斥
此刻的花朵
那使青春骄傲的夜
抱着石头滚动
击碎梦中的玻璃

我为何在此逗留？
中年的书信传播着
浩大的哀怨
从不惑之鞋倒出
沙子，或计谋

没有任何准备
在某次会议的陈述中
我走得更远
沿着一个虚词拐弯
和鬼魂们一起
在歧路迎接日落

ON THE WRONG ROAD

days gone-by rail against
the moment's flower
night that does youth proud
tumbles hugging stones
breaking glass in dreams

why linger on here?
mid-life letters circulate
vast sorrows
shoes of certainty pour out
sand, or schemes

completely unprepared
I walk further out
in some statement at a conference
tracing the twist in a preposition
joining ghosts
on the wrong road to greet sunset

明 镜

夜半饮酒时
真理的火焰发疯
回首处
谁没有家
窗户为何高悬

你倦于死
道路倦于生
在那火红的年代
有人昼伏夜行
与民族对弈

并不止于此
挖掘你睡眠的人
变成蓝色
早晨倦于你
明镜倦于词语

想想爱情
你有如壮士
惊天动地之处
你对自己说
太冷

BRIGHT MIRROR

in the midnight hour of wine
the flame of truth gets crazy
a place for looking back
who has no home
why do windows loom so high

you're tired of death
the road's tired of life
in those flame-red times
someone rests by day and travels by night
playing chess with a nation

but that's not all
people excavating your sleep
turn blue
morning's tired of you
the bright mirror's tired of words

think about love
and you're like some hero
where heaven trembles and earth shakes
you say to yourself
too cold

早晨

那些鱼内脏如灯
又亮了一次

醒来，口中含盐
好似初尝喜悦

我出去散步
房子学会倾听

一些树转身
某人成了英雄

必须用手势问候
鸟和打鸟的人

MORNING

those fish entrails as if lights
blink again

waking, there's salt in my mouth
just like the first taste of joy

I go out for a walk
houses learning to listen

a few trees turn around
and someone's become a hero

you must use hand gestures to greet
birds and the hunters of birds

无 题

行人们点亮自己
脑袋里的灯泡
大街奔向十月的狂想

向一只狗致敬
影子斜向它的经验

泉水暴露了
风景以下的睡眠
我们轮流伏在
长明的窗下哭泣

李白击鼓而歌
从容不迫

UNTITLED

pedestrians lighting their own
light-bulb minds
the street heads for october's wild ideas

in tribute to a dog
shadow leans toward its experience

spring water's laid bare
the sleep underlying landscapes
we take turns hiding beneath
windows of endless light weeping

Li Po beats a drum and sings
calm and unhurried

新手

新手的夜晚
无所畏惧
他们在房顶齐声朗读
一纸无字的黄昏
他们在大雪的债务
和马的喘息中
接近开花的地点
他们在时代广场上
著书立说
用长鞭触及意义
在水泥裂缝
种自己的名字

日子被折叠起来
还剩下什么
随生死起伏的歌声
必将返回到他们
张大而无声的嘴巴中

NOVICE

novice evenings
nothing to fear
they recite on rooftops in one voice
that page of wordless twilight
out on snowstorm debts
and the gasping of tired horses
they approach a site that's blooming
and out on that town square of the age
they produce books and schools of thought
use long whips to touch meanings
sow their names
along cracks in the concrete

days get folded up
what remains
the song tracing life's rise and fall
returns inevitably to their
gaping mouths of silence

重影

谁在月下敲门
看石头开花
琴师在回廊游荡
令人砰然心动
不知朝夕
流水和金鱼
拨动时光方向

向日葵受伤
指点路径
盲人们站在
不可理解之光上
抓住愤怒
刺客与月亮
一起走向他乡

SEEING DOUBLE

who knocks on a door in moonlight
watching stone bloom
a musician wanders the corridors
it makes your heart pound
not knowing if it's morning or night
flowing water and goldfish
adjust the direction of time

a wounded sunflower
points the way
the blind stand on
light beyond understanding
clutching anger
assassin and moon
walk toward a foreign land

领 域

今夜始于何处
客人们在墙上干杯
妙语与灯周旋

谁苦心练习
演奏自己的一生
那秃头钢琴家
家里准有一轮太阳

模仿沉默
我的手爬过桌子

有人把狗赶进历史
再挖掘出来
它们把住大门
一对老人转身飞走
回头时目光凶狠

二月召来乡下木匠
重新支撑天空
道路以外的春天
让人忙于眺望

REALM

where did tonight begin
guests toast the wall
their wit sparring light

practicing relentlessly
to perform his own life
the bald pianist
clearly keeps a full sun at home

imitating silence
my hand crawls across the desk

people chase dogs into history
then excavate
and make them gatekeepers
an old couple turns and hurries away
looking back with a savage gaze

february summons country carpenters
to prop up the sky anew
and springtime beyond the road
keeps us busy with the long view

据我所知

前往那故事中的人们
搬开了一座大山
他才诞生

我从事故出发
刚抵达另一个国家
颠倒字母
使每餐必有意义

掂脚够着时间的刻度
战争对他还太远
父亲又太近
他低头通过考试
踏上那无边的甲板

隔墙有耳
但我要跟上他的速度
写作!

他用红色油漆道路
让凤凰们降落
展示垂死的动作
那些含义不明的路标
环绕着冬天
连音乐都在下雪

AS FAR AS I KNOW

people on the way to that story
moved a mountain
then he was born

setting out from the accident
I barely reached another country
turning alphabets upside down
to fill every meal with meaning

he reaches up to the scale measuring time
war remains too far away
father too close
he stoops to pass through exams
and boards that boundless boatdeck

someone's listening behind walls
I must hurry to keep up with him
writing!

he paints the road red
lets phoenixes land
flaunting death throes
those incoherent roadsigns
surround winter
snow falling even from music

我小心翼翼
每个字下都是深渊

当一棵大树
平息着八面来风
他的花园
因妄想而荒芜

我漫不经心地翻看
他的不良记录
只能坚信过去的花朵

他伪造了我的签名
而长大成人
并和我互换大衣
以潜入我的夜
搜寻着引爆故事的
导火索

I'm careful very careful
there's an abyss beneath every word

when a huge tree
quiets wind from the eight directions
his flower garden
goes to seed for fantasy

I leaf carelessly through
his bad record
nothing to believe but the past's flower

he forged my signature
and grew into a man
traded coats with me
and stole into my night
searching out the story's detonation
fuse

主题

早晨的碗
一生中的朋友
让我回味那种恩惠
而我被门所否认

关于生活会另有解释
很多书在鼓掌
并追随阴郁的革命
埋藏着狐狸骨头

我向西再向东
回避着主题
夜的滑翔机展开
序曲中交错的目光

风景依旧
那群逃税的大象狂奔
政策背道而驰
农民们洗耳恭听

岁月起伏的地方
我摸索着回家
楼上有人打开窗户
泼出了一盆脏水

THEME

a morning bowl
lifelong friend
lets me savor such kindness
and yet doors deny me

there will be other ways of explaining life
many books are applauding
they follow the dismal revolution
burying fox bones

I head west and then east
avoiding the theme
the sailplane of night opening out
crisscross glances in the overture

same scenery as ever
that herd of tax-evading elephants runs wild
official policy hurries in the opposite direction
peasants clean their ears and listen politely

where years rise and fall
I grope my way home
someone upstairs opens a window
and empties a pan of dirty water

守　夜

月光小于睡眠
河水穿过我们的房间
家具在哪儿靠岸

不仅是编年史
也包括非法的气候中
公认的一面
使我们接近雨林
哦哭泣的防线

玻璃镇纸读出
文字叙述中的伤口
多少黑山挡住了
一九四九年

在无名小调的尽头
花握紧拳头叫喊

NIGHTWATCH

moonlight smaller than sleep
the river flows through our room
where is furniture docking

not only annals of history
but also the illicit climate's
acknowledged aspects
bring us to rain forests
o line of defense in tears

glass paperweights decode
writing's wound of narration
how many black mountains blocked
1949

where a nameless tune ends
blossoms scream clenched fists

无 题

——给Martin Mooij

集邮者们窥视生活
欢乐一闪而过

夜傲慢地跪下
托起世代的灯火

风转向，鸟发狂
歌声摇落多少苹果

不倦的情人白了头
我俯身看命运

泉水安慰我
在这无用的时刻

UNTITLED

—for Martin Mooij

stamp collectors peer at life
happiness a flash suddenly gone

arrogant night kneels down
holding up the lights of generations

winds shifts direction, birds crazed
song shaking down how many apples

the hair of tireless lovers turned white
I bend down to look at fate

springwater comforts me
in such useless moments

无 题

人们赶路，到达
转世，隐入鸟之梦
太阳从麦田逃走
又随乞丐返回

谁与天比高
那早天的歌手
在气象图里飞翔
掌灯冲进风雪

我买了份报纸
从日子找回零钱
在夜的入口处
摇身一变

被颂扬之鱼
穿过众人的泪水
喂，上游的健康人
到明天有多远

UNTITLED

people hurry on, arrive
return in another life, fade into bird dreams
the sun flees wheat fields
then comes back trailing after beggars

who's rivaled sky for height
that singer who died young
soars in the weather map
flies into snowstorms holding a lamp

I bought a newspaper
got change back from the day
and at the entrance to night
eased into a new identity

celebrated fish
move through everyone's tears
hey, you folks upstream achievers so hale and hearty
how far is it to tomorrow

夜

充满细节的排浪
我们以外之光
正是想象来自伤口
月亮护士穿行
为每颗心上发条

我们笑了
在水中摘下胡子
从三个方向记住风
自一只蝉的高度
看寡妇的世界

夜比所有的厄运
更雄辩
夜在我们脚下
这遮蔽诗的灯罩
已经破碎

NIGHT

surf crowded with detail
the light beyond us
it's imagination come of wounds
nurse moon meanders
winding each heart's mainspring

we laughed
pulled off beards in the water
remembered wind in three directions
and from the altitude of a cicada
watched the widow's world

night's more eloquent than
all bad fortune
night under our feet
this lampshade over the poem
already shattered

紫色

明亮的下午
号角阵阵
满树的柿子晃动
如知识在脑中
我开门等夜
在大师的时间里
读书，下棋
有人从王位上
扔出石头

没有击中我
船夫幽灵般划过
波光创造了你
并为你纹身
我们手指交叉
一颗星星刹住车
照亮我们

PURPLE

bright afternoon
the bugle call over and over
persimmons filling trees shimmer
like knowledge in the mind
I open the door to await night
and in a sage-master's time
read books, play chess
someone on a throne
throws a rock

doesn't hit me
spectral boatmen row past
ripple-light creates you
etches your skin
our fingers intertwine
a star puts on the brakes
shines all over us

山中一日

九月向西
虚无的鸽子向东
光和马的细腿
在抄着近路
尝遍种子而无梦
我在向阳坡
练习飞翔
仅仅为了沉睡

为了醒来
钟敲十二下
午夜落叶
白昼生烟

A DAY IN THE MOUNTAINS

september heads west
the dove of nothingness heads east
thin legs of light and horses
are taking a shortcut
having tasted every seed and without dreams
I use a sunlit slope
to practice soaring
if only for sleep

for waking
the clock strikes twelve
midnight drops its leaves
daylight smolders

无 题

几度诗中回首
夜鸟齐鸣
你向歌声逝去之处
释放着烟雾

打伞进入明天
你，漫游者
从你的尽头再向前
什么能替代喜悦

世纪的狐狸们
在鸿沟之间跳跃
你看见那座辉煌的桥
怎样消失在天边

一个早晨触及
核桃隐秘的思想
水的激情之上
是云初醒时的孤独

UNTITLED

looking back a few times in the poem
night birds singing together
you set smoke drifting free
toward a place where song vanishes

walking into tomorrow beneath an umbrella
you, a wanderer
set out from your own end
what can replace joy

the century's foxes
leap from abyss to abyss
you see how that glorious bridge
dissappears at the sky's edge

morning touches
the secret thought of a walnut
above the passion of water
it's the loneliness of cloud waking

旧 地

死亡总是从反面
观察一幅画

此刻我从窗口
看见我年轻时的落日
旧地重游
我急于说出真相
可在天黑前
又能说出什么

饮过词语之杯
更让人干渴
与河水一起援引大地
我在空山倾听
吹笛人内心的呜咽

税收的天使们
从画的反面归来
从那些镀金的头颅
一直清点到落日

OLD PLACES

death's always on the other side
watching the painting

at the window just now
I saw a sunset from my youth
visiting old places again
I'm anxious to tell the truth
but before the skies go dark
what more can be said

drinking a cup of words
only makes you thirstier
I join riverwater to quote the earth
and listen in empty mountains
to the flute player's sobbing heart

angels collecting taxes
return from the painting's other side
from those gilded skulls
taking inventory clear into sunset

局外人

一代人如帷幕落下
下一代人在鼓掌

置身于暗处的人
你经历的时间
正得到重视
摸索，于是有光
让一半生命空出来
充满鹤鸣

有人在病中游泳
当秋风察看
幼兽小小的脾气
道路加入睡眠
在打败你的光线中
你坚守无名栅栏

OUTSIDER

one generation drops like a curtain
the next is applauding

the lifetime you've known
hiding in dark places
starts gaining attention
groping, hence light
letting half a life empty out
and fill with crane song

someone's swimming in sickness
as autumn wind inspects
the small temperaments of young animals
the road joins sleep
and in radiant light that's defeated you
you stand fast at the nameless fence

下一棵树

风从哪儿来
我们数着罂粟籽中的
日日夜夜

大雪散布着
某一气流的谎言
邮筒醒来
信已改变含义
道路通向历史以外
我们牵回往事
拴在下一棵树上

来吧，野蛮人
请加入这一传说
这预订的时刻开花
谦卑的火焰
变成他乡之虎

我们游遍四方
总是从下一棵树出发
返回，为了命名
那路上的忧伤

THE NEXT TREE

where is it wind comes from
we count days and nights passing
inside poppy seeds

a huge snowstorm spreads
that lie a certain flow of air tells
a mailbox wakes
letters already meaning something else
the road leads somewhere beyond history
we shepherd old memories out
and hitch them to the next tree

come, you barbarians
please join this legend
this moment reserved in advance blooms
humble flames
becoming a tiger in a foreign land

we've traveled everywhere
always setting out from the next tree
and returning, just to name
that sorrow of the road

为 了

不眠之灯引导着你
从隐蔽的棋艺中
找到对手

歌声兜售它的影子
你从某个结论
走向开放的黎明
为什么那最初的光线
让你如此不安?

一颗被种进伤口的
种子拒绝作证:
你因期待而告别
因爱而受苦

激情，正如轮子
因闲置而完美

FOR THE PURPOSE OF

a sleepless lamp leads you
to search out an opponent
in the hidden art of chess

song peddles its shadow
from a certain conclusion
you walk toward the opening dawn
why is it the earliest gleam
makes you so anxious?

a seed planted inside wounds
refuses to bear witness
you leave whenever you expect more
suffer whenever you love

passion, just like a wheel
grows perfect whenever it's idle

无题

当语言发疯，我们
在法律的一块空地上
因聋哑而得救
一辆辆校车
从光的深渊旁驶过
夜是一部旧影片
琴声如雨浸润了时代

孤儿们追逐着蓝天
服丧的书肃立
在通往阐释之路上
杜鹃花及姐妹们
为死亡而开放

UNTITLED

when language was insane, we
stood in the law's one vacant lot
and being deaf and dumb were saved
one school bus after another
skirts past an abyss of light
night's an old movie
and music soaks into the age like rain

as orphans chase azure skies
books stand in mourning
on the road leading to explanation
azalea and her sisters
bloom for death

失　眠

你在你的窗外看你
一生的光线变幻

因嫉妒而瞎了眼
星星逆风而行
在死亡的隐喻之外
展开道德的风景

在称为源泉的地方
夜终于追上了你
那失眠的大军
向孤独的旗帜致敬

辗转的守夜人
点亮那朵惊恐之花
猫纵身跃入长夜
梦的尾巴一闪

INSOMNIA

you see yourself outside your window
a lifetime's gleam in flux

gone blind out of jealousy
stars sail against the wind
beyond death's metaphor
and unfold ethical landscapes

in what is called a place of wellsprings
night finally catches up to you
that army of insomnia
salutes the flag of solitude

a nightwatchman tossing and turning
lights up that terror-blossom
a cat leaps into endless night
the dream's tail flashing once

零度以上的风景

是鹞鹰教会歌声游泳
是歌声追溯那最初的风

我们交换欢乐的碎片
从不同的方向进入家庭

是父亲确认了黑暗
是黑暗通向经典的闪电

哭泣之门砰然关闭
回声在追赶它的叫喊

是笔在绝望中开花
是花反抗着必然的旅程

是爱的光线醒来
照亮零度以上的风景

LANDSCAPE OVER ZERO

it's hawk teaching song to swim
it's song tracing back to the first wind

we trade scraps of joy
enter family from different directions

it's a father confirming darkness
it's darkness leading to that lightning of the classics

a door of weeping slams shut
echoes chasing its cry

it's a pen blossoming in lost hope
it's a blossom resisting the inevitable route

it's love's gleam waking to
light up landscape over zero

故事

少年的喇叭盲目的回声
饮水的城市吐露真情
专家们攀登着夜的高压电
警察只出现过一次
在毫无意义的笑声中

语法里的狗叫浪的叹息
电话亭在海边做梦
一条鱼一种理由召来风暴
管风琴冒着烟流星飞溅
颂扬的是死去的一年

我沿着主要情节线
到达作者开始构思的地方
泪水中看见酒后的太阳
油漆未干的四月
蜂群引导饥饿的意象

STORY

children's trumpet blind echo
a water-drinking city tells the truth
experts climb night's high voltage
police appeared only once
in meaningless laughter

grammar's inner bark tidal sighs
a phonebooth dreams beside the sea
a fish a reason summoning storms
a pipe-organ smokes meteors spatter
what's praised is a dead year

I follow the main plot
to where an author's conception began
see a drunken sun through tears
wet-paint April
bees leading out images of hunger

不对称

历史的诡计之花开放
忙于演说的手指受伤
攒下来的阳光成为年龄
你沉于往事和泡沫
埋葬愤怒的工具
一个来自过去的陌生人
从镜子里指责你

而我所看到的是
守城的昏鸦正一只只死去
教我呼吸和意义的老师
在我写作的阴影咳血
那奔赴节日的衣裙
随日蚀或完美的婚姻
升起，没有歌声

ASYMMETRY

the blossom of history's ruse opens
fingers busy with talk are wounded
hoarded sunlight becomes age
you drown in times past and bubbles
bury anger's tools
a stranger out of the past
chides you from the mirror

though what I've seen is
the city's dusky guardian-crows dying one by one
and those who taught me breath and meaning
coughing up blood in shadows my writing casts
dresses rushing toward holidays
follow solar eclipse and perfect marriage
& rise, songless

蜡

青春期的蜡
深藏在记忆的锁内
火焰放弃了酒
废墟上的匆匆过客
我们的心

我们的心
会比恨走得更远
夜拒绝明天的读者
被点燃的蜡烛
晕眩得象改变天空的
一阵阵钟声
此刻唯一的沉默

此刻唯一的沉默
是裸露的花园
我们徒劳地卷入其中
烛火比秋雾更深
漫步到天明

WAX

puberty's wax
hidden deep in the lock of memory
flame abandoned wine
passersby hurrying over the ruins
our hearts

our hearts
can go further than hate
night refuses tomorrow's reader
lit candlewax
dizzy as sky-altering
bells tolling over and over
the moment's only silence

the moment's only silence
is a naked flower garden
we're caught up in it for nothing
candle-flame deeper than autumn fog
strolling into dawn

关键词

我的影子很危险
这受雇于太阳的艺人
带来最后的知识
是空的

那是蛀虫工作的
黑暗属性
暴力的最小的孩子
空中的足音

关键词，我的影子
锤打着梦中之铁
踏着那节奏
一只孤狼走进

无人失败的黄昏
鹭鸶在水上书写
一生一天一个句子
结 束

KEYWORD

my shadow's dangerous
this craftsman the sun hired
brings final knowledge
it's empty

that's the dark nature of
a moth's hungry work
smallest child of violence
footsteps in air

keyword my shadow
hammers dreamworld iron
stepping to that rhythm
a lone wolf walks into

dusk of no one's defeat
an egret writes on water
a life a day a sentence
ends

无 题

千百个窗户闪烁
这些预言者
在昨天与大海之间
哦迷途的欢乐

桥成为现实
跨越公共的光线
而涉及昨日玫瑰的
秘密旅行提供
一张纸一种困境

母亲的泪我的黎明

UNTITLED

windows glimmer by the thousand
these prophets
between yesterday and the sea
o that joy of losing the way

a bridge becomes reality
spanning the public's gleam
and the clandestine journey involving
yesterday's rose offers
a sheet of paper a dilemma

mother's tears my daybreak

远 景

海鸥，尖叫的梦
抗拒着信仰的天空
当草变成牛奶
风失去细节

若风是乡愁
道路就是其言说

在道路尽头
一只历史的走狗
扮装成夜
正向我逼近

夜的背后
有无边的粮食
伤心的爱人

THE LONG VIEW

seagulls, shriek dream
resisting skies of belief
when pasture becomes milk
wind loses detail

if wind is the longing for home
roads must be its speech

at the far end of the road
history's stooge
masquerades as night
and closes in on me

out back of night
it's boundless grain
heartbreak lover

边　境

风暴转向北方的未来
病人们的根在地下怒吼
太阳的螺旋桨
驱赶蜜蜂变成光芒
链条上的使者们
在那些招风耳里播种

被记住的河流
不再终结
被偷去了的声音
已成为边境

边境上没有希望
一本书
吞下一个翅膀
还有语言的坚冰中
赎罪的兄弟
你为此而斗争

BORDERS

storms turn toward the north's future
sick people's roots howl underground
a sun propeller
chases bees until they're rays of light
messengers in chains
sow seed in those ears long for the wind

remembered rivers
never end
stolen sound
becomes borders

borders allow no hope
a book
swallows a wing
and still in the hard ice of language
a brother redeeming his crimes
you struggle on for this

借来方向

一条鱼的生活
充满了漏洞
流水的漏洞啊泡沫
那是我的言说

借来方向
醉汉穿过他的重重回声
而心是看家狗
永远朝向抒情的中心

行进中的音乐
被一次事故所粉碎
天空覆盖我们
感情生活的另一面

借来方向
候鸟挣脱了我的睡眠
闪电落入众人之杯
言者无罪

BORROWING A DIRECTION

a fish's life
is full of loopholes
streamwater's loopholes ah bubbles
that's my way of speaking

borrowing a direction
the drunk passes through his echoes layer by layer
but the heart's a watchdog
forever facing the lyric's essence

music driving forward
gets shattered in the accident
skies cover the other
side of our emotional life

borrowing a direction
migratory birds break out of my sleep
lightning strikes everyone's cup
the speaker's innocent

新 年

怀抱花朵的孩子走向新年
为黑暗文身的指挥啊
在倾听那最短促的停顿

快把狮子关进音乐的牢笼
快让石头伴装成隐士
在平行之夜移动

谁是客人？当所有的日子
倾巢而出在路上飞行
失败之书博大精深

每一刻都是捷径
我得以穿过东方的意义
回家，关上死亡之门

NEW YEAR

a child carrying flowers walks toward the new year
a conductor tattooing darkness
listens to the shortest pause

hurry a lion into the cage of music
hurry stone to masquerade as a recluse
moving in parallel nights

who's the visitor? when the days all
tip from nests and fly down roads
the book of failure grows boundless and deep

each and every moment's a shortcut
I follow it through the meaning of the East
returning home, closing death's door

无 题

醒来是自由
那星辰之间的矛盾

门在抵抗岁月
丝绸卷走了叫喊
我是被你否认的身分
从心里关掉的灯

这脆弱的时刻
敌对的岸
风折叠所有的消息
记忆变成了主人

哦陈酒
因表达而变色
煤会遇见必然的矿灯
火不能为火作证

UNTITLED

in waking there is freedom
that contradiction among stars

doors resisting the years
silk carried screams away
I'm the identity you deny
lamp switched off in the heart

this fragile moment
hostile shores
wind folds up all the news
memory's become master

o vintage wine
changing color for clear expression
coal meets the miner's inevitable lamp
fire cannot bear witness to fire

冬之旅

谁在虚无上打字
太多的故事
是十二块石头
击中表盘
是十二只天鹅
飞离冬天

而夜里的舌头
描述着光线
盲目的钟
为缺席者呼喊

进入房间
你看见那个丑角
在进入冬天时
留下的火焰

WINTER TRAVELS

who's typing on the void
too many stories
they're twelve stones
hitting the clockface
twelve swans
flying out of winter

tongues in the night
describe gleams of light
blind bells
cry out for someone absent

entering the room
you see that jester's
entered winter
leaving behind flame

否认

蒙面的纪念日
是一盏灯笼
收割从夜开始
到永恒

从死者的眼里
采摘棉花
冬天索回记忆
纺出十年长的风

日子成为路标
风叩响重音之门
果园没有历史
梦里没有医生

逃离纪念日
我呼吸并否认

deny

that a veiled anniversary
is a lantern
harvest begins at night
keeps on into forever

plucking cotton
from the eyes of the dead
winter demands memory's return
spinning out a decade-long wind

days become road signs
wind knocks at the gate of accented sounds
orchards have no history
dreams have no doctors

fleeing the anniversary
I breathe and deny

休 息

你终于到达
云朵停靠的星期天

休息，正如谎言
必须小心有人窥看

它在键盘上弹奏
白昼与黑夜

弹奏明天
那幸福的链条

死者挣脱了影子
锁住天空

REST

you finally arrive
at the sunday where clouds moor

rest, just like a lie
make sure no one's watching

it's performing on a keyboard
days white and nights black

performing tomorrow
that chain of happiness

the dead broke free of shadow
and locked up the sky

工作

与它的影子竞赛
鸟变成了回声

并非偶然，你
在风暴中选择职业
是飞艇里的词
古老的记忆中的
刺

开窗的母亲
象旧书里的主人公
展开秋天的折扇
如此耀眼

你这不肖之子
用白云擦洗玻璃
擦洗玻璃中的自己

WORK

competing with its shadow
a bird becomes echo

not unexpectedly, you
choosing a profession in the storm
are the word inside zeppelins
ancient memory's
thorn

mother opening windows
like some hero in an old book
spreads autumn's fan open
dazzling the eyes

you unfilial son
wiping glass clean with white cloud
wiping the you in glass clean

旅 行

那影子在饮水
那笑声模仿
撑开黎明的光线的
崩溃方式

带着书去旅行
书因旅行获得年龄
因旅行而匿名
那深入布景的马
回首

你刚好到达
那人出生的地方

鱼从水下看城市
水下有新鲜的诱饵
令人难堪的锚

JOURNEY

that shadow's drinking water
laughter mimics
the dawn-opening gleam's
collapsing ways

you set out on a journey with books
books age because of journeys
hide their names because of journeys
that horse deep in the stage scenery
turns its head

you've just arrived
at that person's birthplace

fish watch the city from underwater
among fresh bait underwater
there's an embarrassing anchor